New Age Philosophy

to plan

TOMORROW AS THE BEST DAY YOU'LL EVER HAVE

New Age Philosophy

New Age Philosophy

by

William Carroll

ISBN 0-910390-90-8
Copyright 2012

Published by

Coda Publications
P.O. Box 2100
McKinleyville
California 95519

Foreword

Many will ignore this book as it does not contain contrived limitations about living within our complicated world of today. For here is New Age Philosophy, the merging of Mind, Body and Spirit to enhance potential joys of life without borders or confining dogma.

More than 350 aphorisms fill the following pages, There's no Table of Contents, Index, or Chapters, to influence your selection of those most helpful. But enjoy this book slowly for you'll find there are a number of obtuse "thinkers" to puzzle over. And skip beyond less complicated others which do not blend with your future.

For you, and you alone, are the only person who can plan tomorrow as The Best Day You'll Ever Have. From birth to death, our critical choice is how we live.

Excuses won't help. Knowledge will.

Read with care to find the winning aphorisms you could use to be happier and achieve your desires . . . after making just one decision.

Where are you going?

William Carroll

The author of this volume, William Carroll, was born in San Francisco in 1915 and currently lives a comfortable and productive life in Northern California.

He has written over 50 books and published a total near 150. As an internationally known photographer and journalist, his travels have taken him into China, New Zealand, a few of the Pacific islands, around much of Europe, the United Kingdom, Ireland, nearly all of the United States, Mexico, Central America, Panama and all the nations, but Paraguay, of South America.

From such, and the many friends, he distilled this approach to New Age Philosophy that enhances the potential of modern living.

Enjoy his sharing for that is what this book is all about.

Body mind and soul are one, which is contrary to

the societal disintegation we now face

Accordingly tomorrow is the best day you'll ever

have to do it all better

Here's how

New Age

Tomorrow is the day that arrives brand new

A day all of us can use more of

Tomorrow is an opportunity to do today better

Where you can get it all together.

For when there is no Tomorrow, that is a Destiny

from which you cannot escape

This is your book about living with joy

New Age

New age philosophy is for living a life

that's really your own

With a philosophy of happiness

Where the only value of an ar guement

is to bring peace

New Age

And saying "Yes" opens more doors than

mumbling "No"

These are thinkers

you may have to consider slowly

Enjoy living a life that's really your own

New Age

"I"'d rather be wrong than unhappy"

is freedom to do your best

Sitting with an empty brain

won't get you anywhere

Want less, live more

New Age

Gratitude has a short memory

Live with joy. It's a lot more fun

Chum for new opportunities

as you would chum for more fish

New Age

Depleting friends defines you

If the well is empty, go elsewhere.

Disappear for a while and emer ge a better new

New Age

Some will try to manage your life.......their way

An imaginary rose never blooms,

nor will a one-sided love af fair

Refuel yourself or coast downhill on empty

New Age

If you are always right, where are your friends?

Perfection is an ideal only found within your

imagination

A true lover gives you a hand, not a mandate

New Age

Picking boogers is a useless pastime

Love can enhance or be the excuse to demean

When you won't see the door

you can't go anywhere

New Age

Falling in love

could be the same as being tripped and trashed

Thoughtless burdens overwhelm

the warmest heart

A fresh relationships is opportunity ,

not rehabilitation

New Age

To live well, live well

Roses seldom grow in a weed patch.

Get out.

Think of everything then select carefully what
you consider the best

New Age

When you get all you want, something is wrong

You do not have to consider it right,

for it to be good

Excess money is a worry not a happiness.

New Age

Work can be pleasure if you make it so

Walking away is far better

than being carried out

What's wrong may be more your imagination

than fact

New Age

The best ideas are from a mind, not a committee

Objectives always include consequences

The value of thinking includes the value

of not doing

New Age

The belly-button knows little about love

Shouting submerges vision

What you see in the future

could be near enough to achieve

New Age

It may not hurt to think twice and move once

Knowing what you want

is half the wisdom of getting it

Learn the rules before you play the game

New Age

A never-changing smile isn't

A better life is okay

if you know what to do with it

A love affair takes two

New Age

Results of an idea are more important

than details of the initiative

Honesty is as good as it gets

Is there another way? Look!

New Age

A tired heart values a fresh vision

What's funny may not be

Doing a good job is not enough

for it must meet the need.

New Age

Disappointments are okay

because tomorrow is another day

Alone is not lonely unless you allow it to be so

Thoughtful personal criticism is priceless:

Once.

New Age

A drippy nose needs a hanky, not a long tongue

If you fail often, find other ways

Look around to see what you may be missing

New Age

Remember that yesterday was practice for today

which is practice for your better tomorrow

Worry drains the steam out of every boiler

Using notes unclutters the mind

New Age

A nicer way pleases two: You and the other

True success arrives in modest portions

Live a life others will envy

New Age

Last years clothes should always fit

There's nothing wrong with pride in what you do

Even Greek gods lived on high

New Age

Friends and enemies are the same

with different opinions

Arguments instruct or depress

for only you know the truth.

Constant negativity is self-destruction of your

future

New Age

Don't reject being wrong, for maybe you are

Warning: Exercise of the brain brings happiness

Marriage is not a bad idea

when it merges the sharings of two

New Age

"Better around the corner"

merits looking before turning

Self-evident truths are not always the best answer

When you believe everything you are told:

"Watch out!"

New Age

Why is it that only one religious leader

is pictured smiling?

Take care of yourself

for you are the best you'll ever have

Existing is only the basement foundation

of living

New Age

Friending is more fun than fighting.

The road to hell is paved with good intentions

Think twice.

New Age

Anger has little to do with wisdom

Use it or lose it

Get past today's mistakes and move on wiser

New Age

Misdirecting an adversary

is often a useful defense

A fine relationship

is the pairing of compatible futures

That new tomorrow

will be everything you make it

New Age.

What you think is who you are

Depression and hiding

have little to do with living

If you are going to be bad

enjoy being good at it

New Age

There's nothing wrong with being better

Pretending you're a nice person

could become a permanent asset

Having what you want merits continued care

New Age

When not sure where you are

stop and look around carefully

Some should use toilet paper

to wipe dribble off their chin

To find a better way, select from better ways

New Age :

A dream team can be as many as two

A friend's opinion is great

if you're careful how you use it

Divergents do not a happy pair make

New Age

More is less when its value is hidden

It's not wrong to offer help

as long as you don't insist

Listen to an enemy for priceless knowledge

New Age 1

One-way streets, and one-way minds,

offer little chance for change

There is no love that does not end with a parting

The numbers of age mean less than the attitude

New Age

A sincere "Thank You" defines your worth

To explore a woman know her dif ferently,

every time ——— often

If you are emotional, use the good ones

New Age

Insistence and resistance

are mutually destructive

Words of wisdom are opportunities,

seldom blind alleys

To become a nicer person: Practice now

New Age

Complaints work best

when presented as compliments

Thinking and doing work well hand in hand

Instant decisions are to avoid harm,

seldom to choose a future

New Age

Trip a friend and you may be the one to fall

Value Grandmother 's advice

by the width of Grandfather 's smile

Causing trouble to attract attention

is often more trouble than you're worth.

New Age

A tongue may be as vicious as a sword

Being a smart-ass is more ass than smart

When you can't think clearly

stop and start over later

New Age

Suicide is also an absolute for those left behind

Delay a decision long enough

and you won't have to make it

A new friend is an opportunity to not make the

same mistakes all over again

New Age

What you see in your future

is best when the future is shared

Your greatest relationship

includes tiny measures of gentle firmness

If you are doubtful about what you are going to

say: Don't

New Age

There's good and bad advice,

with your decision the beneficiary

Choose friends like buying shoes:

Both must fit and know where you are going.

A friend in need is a friend indeed.

(A priceless oldie)

New Age

We may settle for second best

to hurry a trashy victory

Silence often says more than words

Know your lover as you know yourself

New Age

A teener's dream: Fast cars and slow girls

With 10,000 excuses

we often try to hide the obvious

One - A - Day: Good deeds that is

New Age

If there's another way to be wrong

keep talking and you'll hear it

Your mother was always right:

She had you. Be happy

Being a good friend is impossible

if you dislike yourself.

New Age

Holding a happy child

changes everything for the better

Be greedy.

Make tomorrow another day of success

If love is so important, why does it fade so easily?

New Age.

Try thinking — it will help

Random acts of kindness enhance two

Children reflect their parents for good or bad

New Age

Tomorrow is where you have it made

if you try

Good luck is better than rising early

A friend without a heart is an enemy in disguise

New Age]

You can't weave rope from sand of the sea

God helps those who help themself

....and others too

A head without knowledge is harm on the way

New Age

There is no home like your heart

A selfish friend always needs

The generous seldom go to hell

New Age

Seek more than you deserve

and treasure its arrival

Happiness always contains

small measures of sorrow

Enjoy the pleasure of doing your best

New Age

Life waits for no man

What you take without thought

is lost without wisdom.

Great minds often live apart,

as mountains and rivers are never one

New Age

There is little good judgment

within overly enthusastic love af fairs

It should be just enough to have what you need

Wisdom is seldom shouted

New Age

A second thought should have been first

Don't bother to question

what you have no need to know

Women are protected by convenient memories

New Age

Be the Wizard of Ahs

for your personal partner

Do the best you can

for that's the best there is

Those of established quality

merit your thoughtful attention

New Age

Think too fast and miss your best opportunities

Being intelligent does not guarantee wisdom

Push a problem too far

and it becomes Mount Everest

New Age]

Encouraging another

is an act of priceless support

Negativity defines you, not the situation

Success merits appreciation of your good luck

New Age

Relax and allow time to gentle the situation

Step aside, for trouble makers are seldom worth

the conflict

Whatever you desire includes consequences

New Age

With nothing good to say, say nothing.

Experience enhances wisdom

Do not criticize what you cannot mend

New Age

Nothing is shorter than time

Today forecasts tomorrow

We are the one causing most of our problems

New Age

You know only today but never into tomorrow

A constantly smiling face

may conceal a deceitful heart

Taking more than you can handle

is always more than you can handle

New Age

A long look ahead beats three looks behind

You cannot learn to fly

if you never leave the nest

A pessimist is seldom changeable

New Age

Being smart is better than being strong

What you believe about life has little reality

The longest road out

may well be the shortest road home

New Age

Fear is as a good a reason to run far away ,

as it is the reason to abandon rage.

An applied decision is more often resented

than valued

Best of all are a kind heart and good life

New Age :

Kiss something often even if it is only an ear

Your interpretation and action are inseparable

Wisdom is a critical asset

New Age

Time used to think first

is time well spent for doing it well

Good advice is worthless

unless you were listening

Blow your nose often to air out the brain

New Age

Boredom may be your problem,

not the speaker 's words

A loving whisper pleasures beyond compare

Your complaints

may be going in the wrong direction

New Age

Try thinking

The mirror may reflect a person that few like.

Look closely

Every problem has a solution,

though you may not like it

New Age

These words are for thinkers,

not mandates for obedience

Give orders with care

or you may be doing it yourself

What you dream may be better for someone else

New Age

You're not expected to like everything here,

just use the ones you do

For as you read, line for line

You'll find things you value little

And every now and then a priceless gem

to change you forever

Because this book is like your life, to accept or

reject as you are

And organize the best tomorrow you've ever had

New Age

A birthday celebrates your mother 's discomfort

Forgive and forget.....the first time

Always be right and enjoy your tears

New Age

Sage includes age

Use experience as payment

for what you really want

Be gentle and enhance the response

New Age

Hot lips are moist caresses

The one at the top has no where else to go

Predict a better Tomorrow and make it happen

New Age

See A Penny

Pick it up,

And throughout the day

Enjoy good luck.

(A happy oldie.)

These aphorisms are more fun and less expensive

than psychiatrists.

Good sex is — just that.

New Age

Peeking into closets only views

what the owner put there.

Brainstorming works best

with more brains than storm.

To view a loving couple

adds another sunrise to the day .

New Age

Seniors have more rights

because they know best what to do with them.

Large friends have much to explore and enjoy .

Children should not

— no matter how old they are.

New Age

Always leave a bit of touching undone;

for tomorrow it could

jump-start another bright day .

A carving on our mantel proclaims :

"In this home there are no enemies"

If at first you dont succeed

rest for about 15 minutes

New Age

Never forget that while it may be possible

to love thy neighbor

all hell breaks loose when you're caught.

Going home alone may be more relaxing

than waking up and wondering "Who?"

Is virtue its own punishment?

New Age

Many dedicated singles are sure theres nothing

wrong with children as long as parents keep then

locked up at home.

No one will ever know your imperfections

until you show them.

One religious theory of creation begins with a

good apple and ripe sex

In our time good apples are hard to find.

New Age

Be sure you know how to add the score

before doing a number.

Thinking before you speak is a great way to

appear much smarter than you are.

Some people are worth ignoring for the same

reason you sidestep a dog's dump.

New Age

Winners always know how to call it quits

The best time to admit that you are too old

is about ten minutes before death

An orgy is a great way to remind yourself that

two's company and more's a mess

New Age

Lust is so far behind Love the dictionary may be
telling us something.

Honor the memory of lost love by opening your
heart for another.

Feels good? Do it!

New Age

There is nice osmosis in frequent hugs.

Why is it we all find time to repeat so many of

our past mistakes?

Do not be so eager or you'll miss all the fun stuf f.

New Age

There is little age on a smiling face.

A lover is who you enjoy.

The person you love is where you share.

Many of us would be unemployed if we paid as

little attention to our work

as we do to making love.

New Age

Look over your shoulder often

for the real you is not far behind.

Rationalization is the art of fabricating

right from wrong.

Delight is finding yourself in another 's heart.

New Age

Being in love is waking up in the morning

and not really caring who you are

The best advice in the world is seldom around

when it does not work

Even the most disagreeable person in the world

may have a virtue; like washing dishes

somewhere else

New Age

Think a nice thing then do it

Passion is delight on fire

If life is okay, don't fix it

New Age

We are taught almost everything

except how to enjoy happiness

There is no such thing as an elegant fart

or acceptable insult

When an older person is asked how they have

sex, the most comforting answer is

"With appreciation"

New Age

Be better than just another good example

Consider looking at your friends as though seeing
them for the first time to decide if you are really
where you should be

Listen carefully to a compulsive talker and you'll
soon hear what theyre trying to hide

New Age

A sullen person is like a bomb

that dares you to light the fuse

Oral sex has nothing to do with humming a love

song while doing the dishes

Wisdom is seldom a blessing of the young and

sometimes we wonder about the rest of us

New Age

Look to the parents if you are interested in seeing

your love's distant future

Once you decide where you are going, join

a fellow traveler instead of burdening yourself

with useless freight

The closest relatives are those you see seldom

and think about often

New Age

If celibacy is the same as being good,

why is there so much delight in being bad?

If fresh air makes the home feel better ,

consider what fresh thinking does for your brain

If you have only two choices: "Y es" or "No",

it is possible "Maybe" should be the decision

New Age

Frequently rising to the occasion is a great way

for men to keep their lady happy

Because you cannot take it with you,

leave a lot of kindness behind

Everyone wants to play God

without the responsibility

New Age]

Merging bellybuttons does not a love make

Every passing is a sadness beyond relief

Politics makes strange bedfellows,

as does booze.

New Age.

The heart always knows of love

the body seldom understands

Finding the hand you are reaching for

makes the entire day worthwhile

Love at first sight may work well

if your luck holds out

New Age

Repeating mistakes indicates intellectual density

The bottom line of a delightful love af fair

always totals two

Finding a penny is success when you deem it so

New Age

Care for a new love as it may be the last one

you'll ever have

Knowledge is the ultimate power

Trash a lover as you would trash yourself

New Age

It's too late to change today

so improve tomorrow

A gentle prayer will make you feel much better

Allow love in your life and enjoy the heady

perfume of flowers blooming in your heart.

New Age

Comfort amid passing time mirrors your peace

Your partner's privacies are best left untouched

Don't break what you can't fix

New Age

All you do and think today

affects your life tomorrow

Warming up is more comrfortable

than freezing down

Select what you will be proud of

New Age

Entertainment for tonight

has little to do with love for tomorrow

If you allow others to manage your life

be not disapointed at the results

Love at first sight?

Clean your glasses and good luck!

New Age

Real communication includes tender touching

Only you will know which of these lines

will take on a life of its own

Go ahead; change the world

After you fix yourself

New Age

New Age philosophy is to better value each other

Manage your life with more skill

than random enthusiams

A gentleman is all that: Gentle

New Age

Open your eyes to better watch what you say

A winning loser walks away smarter

Don't worry

when it's too late to change everything

New Age

Passion is privilege seeking response

We're a product of ourself so do a good job

Mind, body and soul; there should be nothing less

New Age

Smile at the mirror, for you may even like it

Just think twice to do it once

An overnight alliance serves a purpose

seldom a future

New Age

If you can't do it right don't do it at all

Happiness should be a reasonable belief,

not just a casual opinion

Judge another by how they judge you

New Age

What you think is what you are

If your best is not good enough

forget it and move on

Sad memories are best buried

under continuing kindness

New Age

Responding to a hint brings joy to two

Close friends are altered egos

under a different roof

Partners and babies value kindness to mature well

New Age

Ask for what you want

and be noisily happy if it arrives

Something new could begin with you

There's little good luck in not doing anything

New Age

Respond with a smile and let it happen again

Control everything to insure your defeat

Opportunities encourage adoption

not thoughtless challenges

New Age

Adopt an aphorism that's going your way

Being grumpy closes two minds:

Your's and their's

With full power to fix the world,

what would you do?

New Age

Just because we're animals,

you don't have to act like one

Just try smiling. It feels good

Wish the world well

for it needs all the help it can get

New Age]

-

Peace and privacy encourage thoughtful thinking

Add a gentle prayer to the rising smoke

of a fading candle

Death is a sadness for which there is no answer
That is why this book ends with a blank page for
your appointment with Destiny, which
will never be canceled

New Age

New Age

www.ingramcontent.com/pod-product-compliance
Lightning Source LLC
Chambersburg PA
CBHW020913090426
42736CB00008B/622